Loving My Working Mom

by **Dr. Danielle Hyles**   illustrated by **Enrico Iskandar**

Loving My Working Mom

iUniverse books may be ordered through booksellers or by contacting:

iUniverse
1663 Liberty Drive
Bloomington, IN 47403
www.iuniverse.com
1-800-Authors (1-800-288-4677)

Because of the dynamic nature of the Internet, any web addresses or links contained in this book may have changed since publication and may no longer be valid. The views expressed in this work are solely those of the author and do not necessarily reflect the views of the publisher, and the publisher hereby disclaims any responsibility for them.

Any people depicted in stock imagery provided by Getty Images are models, and such images are being used for illustrative purposes only. Certain stock imagery © Getty Images.

ISBN: 978-1-6632-0353-3 (sc)
ISBN: 978-1-6632-0354-0 (e)

Library of Congress Control Number: 2020911271

Print information available on the last page.

iUniverse rev. date: 06/19/2020

To our mothers and mothers everywhere

Who nurture, love, provide and care

We appreciate everything you do

And all the hardships you go through

Dr. D.H. ~ E.I.

My **mom** is a **superhero.** She works all **day** and all **night.**

At **night**,
she puts on her **cape**
and begins to make **dinner**.
Many times, it's my **favourite**.

We look to the **stars**
as she **reads** me a **bedtime story**
and **kisses**
me **goodnight**.

When I ask "again", "again", she will read my book
two or three times,
and even give me another kiss
on my forehead,
and tell me good night.
I know that after I go to sleep
she is still doing
superhero work.
Go Mom!

I woke up **late** one night
and saw her **cleaning** out the coat closet.
That's a **big** job.
Go **Mom**!

"I have **one question** though, Mom.
What do you do in the day at **work?**"
Vivien asked.

"I can tell you
but I will do one **better**.
I am going to take **you**
to work with **me**",
Mom said.

What does Mom
do at work?

She **changed**
right in front of my **eyes.**

It was a **cape,**
no, a **dress,** no, no...
it was a **business suit.**

"Where did the cape go, Mom?" asked Vivien.

Mom answered

"the cape is only there for you to understand

that one day you will grow up and become a Mom too."

"You will **love** your **children** so much that you will want to make sure they grow up with lots of **love** in a warm **home**."

"The cape comes when you are having fun

juggling your house, your work

and the love of your family."

We walked into my Mom's **workplace.**

My **Mom** said,

"this is my **daughter, Vivien.**

She is going to be **learning**

what we do at **work.**"

All day she **showed** me
how to **file** paper in drawers,
answer telephones
and go to **meetings**
with lots of **different** people
doing all different **jobs.**

Our work **fun** day
was **finished**
and we went back **home.**

My working **mom's cape**
came out again and she **cooked**,
cleaned and **loved me**
while **singing** and **dancing** as always
but this time
I grew to really **appreciate** her
for **everything** she does.

About the Author

Dr. Danielle Hyles is a Canadian author with Trinidadian heritage who is currently a school administrator with the Durham Catholic District School Board. She has also written a research-based educational leadership book entitled "Bridging the Opportunity Gap" for educators all over the globe. This book peeks childrens curiosity for careers and supports the home-school parenting pathways connection with a superhero twist of the dual role of mother and worker. For children and parents of all ages.

Printed in the United States
By Bookmasters